I0439403

ALCOHOL
EXPOSED

JOHN CAMPBELL

To my family

for being so supportive and understanding

To the millions of people

who are struggling to overcome the powerful

and damaging effect of alcohol dependency

CONTENTS

ACKNOWLEDGEMENTS

I would like to thank the following organisations for placing the true facts about alcohol into the public domain.

Their excellent work and published documents have been invaluable to me when collecting factual data for this book.

Alcohol Concern

Institute of Alcohol Studies

The Alcohol Health Alliance UK

FOREWORD

Over the past twenty five years I have travelled on a personal journey which, at times, stretched my emotions and survival ability to breaking point. It swallowed up a considerable proportion of my adult life and has significantly changed me as a person.

Before the journey started I was just one of the millions of people who were trying hard to do the best for themselves and their family. I had not really had any break in my employment since I left school and each job I took was better than the one before. My CV was developing quite nicely - reflecting the progress I had made. I was manager of a medium sized company; had three fantastic children, great wife and a nice home. I wasn't the richest man in the world – but I think I was one of the happiest.

Sadly, the bubble dramatically burst and for a long time it felt as if I had stepped outside of my own existence into a different, darker, parallel life. Cutting a very long story short, I had developed an alcohol dependency - and it turned my world upside down. From being a person who enjoyed the odd pint with his friends I became a hopeless alcoholic. I had to leave my job, lost my home and created unbearable grief for my family. I changed from being a lively, outward-going, person who had bundles of friends to a lonely, isolated recluse of a man. From being a confident manager, making important decisions at work, I melted into someone who couldn't decide what colour socks to wear or whether to wear any at all.

The collapse was unbelievably swift.

During the following years I met thousands of people who were in the same 'place' as me. Some of them lost their own battle with life before they had a chance to return to a happier existence. My alcohol dependency has, without doubt, been the hardest thing I have had to deal with in my life – it sucked everything out of my body and left a shell of a person, devoid of charm, character or ambition. Friends dropped away and then faded from my life altogether.

My family suffered the most as they tried in vain to cope with a father and husband who they didn't recognise anymore. One of the most agonising parts of the whole painful process is that I could see what was happening around me but I couldn't seem to do anything to stop it. I had become a captive slave to one of the most powerful drugs in the world. A drug that is widely available and used regularly by a significant proportion of the population. A drug we all know well – alcohol.

During my addictive years under the influence of alcohol I experienced many false dawns and endured endless and sometimes frightening 'home detoxes'. I repeatedly tried to break the drinking pattern in order to gain some hope and respite. But any stability I gained was short-lived and I soon stumbled back into the fog that surrounds dependent drinkers. It almost cost me my life! I knew if I didn't, somehow, force a change I could not expect to live much longer.

Fortunately for me, just when I thought that time was running out, I glimpsed a feint ray of hope through the gloom. For the first time in years I sensed that things could actually change for the better. It was the early and fragile stages of recovery. I had arrived in a long-stay residential 'rehab' service.

Over the next twelve months I embarked on a recovery programme that increasingly gathered momentum - taking me forward to this very day.

The rehabilitation service was designed for people with 'substance misuse' problems - which meant that the residents in the service were dependent on a type of drug; heroin, cocaine, alcohol – it didn't really matter. We all had a history of chronic dependency on one drug or another – some people had multiple drug dependencies.

By that time, of course, my own personal experiences had provided me with a fairly good knowledge of alcohol and how it affected people. Now, I had the unique opportunity to learn about illicit drug use from people whose own lives had been devastated in the same way that mine had. During endless cups of tea, often late into the night, we spoke freely to each other about our lives and how addiction had affected us. I became quite 'clued up' on all aspects of drug use. Like many other substance misuse services there was a wide age-range of residents and, being a 'mixed' unit, we had the benefit of hearing both male and female experiences. It was a learning curve of university standards – even if the chosen subject was extremely personal, painful and emotional to deal with. The common bond that brought us all together at that time in our lives was an instrumental factor in supporting our recovery.

During my time in rehab I began to take a greater interest in the service being provided and in the type of organisation that was delivering it. Finding enough funding to meet the demand for the service was, and still is, a constant challenge. Not every Local Authority, Health Partnership or Social Services department is quick to spend cash on drug dependency services. In recent years, the world's financial mess has had a huge impact on all types of care and support services. Provision and availability of treatment services for alcohol dependency has suffered and long-term residential rehab services are harder to find.

My admiration for the staff team, and their dedicated approach to the job, grew by the day and when my own time at the service was finished I accepted an offer to spend another year working as a volunteer, 3/4 days a week. I had started several projects during my time as a resident and volunteering gave me the opportunity to develop them further. It also became something of an extension to my own recovery. After a year of volunteering I applied for a new post within the service as a project development co-ordinator. I began setting up new training facilities for people who had completed their rehab and needed to get on the employment ladder.

From there I took up a position at the regional office working in fundraising and communications before taking a more specific role within the national quality team. It was a role that would keep me close to the people who were using our services. Their opinions, feedback and ideas were a vital ingredient in the design and development of future service provision. I enjoyed the job tremendously and stayed there for the next twelve years working with over 200 different services across the country and thousands of service users.

Working in the 'Third Sector' or 'Voluntary Sector' was a world apart from my days in private and commercial businesses. I had to adjust fast but, with plenty of help and support, the transition was not too difficult to make. Instead of selling products to keep a business in profit, I was now supporting people who had multiple problems and complex needs. Substance misuse was by far the biggest part of the organisation's work but we also provided a range of services and support for people with mental health problems and learning disabilities – so my learning curve went up another notch. I was already aware of the links between alcohol dependency and mental health problems - my own mental health suffered greatly during my period of alcohol dependency. My introduction to learning disability services was, however, more of a challenge but I must say that it was also one of the most rewarding parts of my new working life.

Over the years I have spent a lot of time with people with alcohol and other drug problems. I saw them at their weakest moments in life, when all seemed dark and lonely - and also at their strongest, as they moved positively towards recovery. I met people who felt that their lives were all but over and then watched as they left the service to get a job, enrol in further education or reunite with a family they thought they had lost forever.

During the early days of my own addiction to alcohol I thought that I was just one of a very small number of people who had lost their way in life. But when I started to work in the substance misuse field I became more aware of the actual scale of the problem. I realised that there was over **1.5 million dependent drinkers** in England alone and **8 million people drinking to levels that will cause them harm.**

I decided to widen my study of alcohol and look at how it affects a modern society. I discovered some alarming facts. This book summarises my thoughts and suggestions, which have been derived both from my own experiences and through extensive research.

You may be happy with the role that alcohol plays in our society or you may, like me, be feeling somewhat concerned. Either way I hope you will find something in the book that will lead you to think further about the role alcohol plays in all of our lives – whether you drink it or not.

John Campbell

INTRODUCTION

Alcohol is generally seen as something that lubricates conversation and helps people to unwind. The marketing of alcoholic drinks is focused on relaxation, leisure activities and social gatherings. It would seem that no event is worthy of any note unless considerable quantities are consumed. It's a cosy message beamed out to reassure the population that drinking alcohol is fun, trendy and cool.

Many drinkers will recognise the marketing message and feel that alcohol has not adversely affected them to any great extent. They will say that it helps them to get through the tough grind of everyday living. However, as I have found to my own personal cost, the reality for millions of other people is very different. If your own drinking is not adversely affecting your health or quality of life - the drinking habits of others will be.

Alcohol has assumed a central role in society, playing a leading part in the lives of people across the nation. It takes up a considerable amount of available leisure time.

Alcohol fashions and influences the behaviour of people - often affecting the way we live our lives. Sadly, it can have a negative impact on;

Physical and mental health
Crime
Family cohesion
Social harmony
Employment
Suicide rates
Road deaths and accidents
Physical and sexual abuse

Alcohol has become a very powerful force and boasts many 'friends' in influential positions. If you raise questions about the impact and the misuse of alcohol in society you run the risk of being frowned upon or berated by those who enjoy alcoholic drinks – often being labelled as a fun-spoiling prohibitionist or worse. Academics and research organisations tend to come under fire if they publish evidence showing the damage caused by alcohol to people's health and the communities they live in. It almost seems as if the act of drinking alcohol is above criticism, sanction or question!

Despite my own painful and frightening experiences of alcohol I'm not actually a prohibitionist. Nevertheless, I am concerned about the central role and elevated position that alcohol claims in the lives of millions of people today. The damage alcohol causes to our health, quality of living and the very fabric of society has now reached alarming levels. Despite mountains of research and enormous quantities of data being produced to show the negative impact of alcohol on the population, our political decision-makers generally choose to ignore it. In my experience, illegal drugs, such as heroin and crack cocaine, do not create anywhere near the same levels of ill-health, social unrest and violence as the legally available drug, alcohol.

Perhaps it is time to seriously examine some home truths and seek solutions to resolving what has become the most significant drug problem in the world today.

THE NEW 'WONDER' DRINK!

Let's consider for a moment that alcoholic drinks have not yet been made available to the general public. The strongest drink available in shops, restaurants and cafes is probably tea, coffee and fresh orange juice.

Imagine that you are the Chief Executive Officer (CEO) of a large food and drinks manufacturer. One of your boffins comes up with a totally new range of drinks that promise to change the way people enjoy themselves. The new drinks, which include varying amounts of alcohol, help people to relax - making their lives seem so much rosier. Consumers will find it easier to unwind after a hard day's toil and the new drinks will be supplied in a range of packaging for parties and social events. In fact the more you consume – the better the party!

As the CEO you will identify the potential for this product and your pulse will be racing as you compute the enormous profits to be made. However, there are guidelines relating to the introduction of new food and drink products and you may worry about obtaining the necessary licence to manufacture and sell the new wonder drink. Not to be deterred your Marketing people come up with a brilliant campaign to get the ball rolling. Government 'watchdogs' are wary at first but when lots of free samples of the product are dispatched to the relevant agencies, with the promise that every sale will trigger a new tax (Duty) paid directly into government coffers, everyone warms to the idea.

After a few more free bottles they are probably even warmer to the idea. Let's also assume, for the sake of this scenario, that the words 'drug' and 'addiction' are never mentioned in the product launch. After many meetings and discussions it is agreed that the new product will be introduced on a two year trial basis. If, after successfully completing the two year trial, there are no adverse results or negative comments from the general public your company will be given a full licence to produce and sell 'Alcoholic drinks' in whatever quantities you like - and anywhere you like.

On completion of the two year trial period a full, independent, report is duly developed for appraisal. The report states that most of the people who tried the new drink thought that it was pretty good and that it did have a marked effect on their lives. It was a good way to relax and unwind and certainly helped to 'break the ice' in a variety of social occasions. People did notice, however, that they needed to buy more and more of the product each month in order to maintain the initial 'feel good' factor. Despite general acceptance that the new product had made a significant impact in its first two years of existence, there were some very disturbing side effects recorded.

For instance, over the two year trial period:

50,000 people actually died *as a result of drinking the new product*

3 million *people were made seriously ill and needed hospital care*

Many people who drank the product created ***violent disturbances*** *on the streets and in their homes*

A&E departments were overflowing *at night and on weekends with people badly injured as a result of drinking the new product or being attacked by someone who had. This stretched the A&E service to breaking point*

Colossal financial pressure was placed on the NHS over the two year trial with budgets drained by some ***£7 billion*** *in treating people who drank the product regularly*

*Many **town centres** had become **'no go' areas** at night due to the threat posed by those drinking the product*

Communities, families and work places were severely disrupted

Employers claimed that absenteeism soared and is still rising

***Violent crimes** (including murder) virtually **doubled** across the country*

*Child abuse incidents increased by over **60%***

***Domestic violence incidents doubled**, with the increase caused directly by drinkers of the new product*

*Following the trial period there are now **over 2 million children at risk** due to one or both of their parents drinking the new product.*

…

I think you will agree that any product causing that level of sickness, death, violence and disorder across the land would be banned instantly. The organisations producing it would probably have to pay out £billions in fines and compensation payments; the directors of the company manufacturing the product may also face lengthy terms in prison for crimes ranging from manslaughter to inciting civil unrest.

The nation's families, communities, health and well-being would have been brought to a new and dangerous level - bordering on collapse.

The reality, of course, is that alcohol has always been here and the statistics are, sadly, genuine!

Alcoholic drinks such as wine and beer have been around for a long time – thousands of years in fact. They would have been part of the staple diet for many families and were often used for medicinal or religious purposes. Most of the wine produced in the Middle Ages was likely to be made by monks on monastery land. They perfected the art of producing fine wines for religious festivals and obviously saw the commercial potential for selling the product within local communities.

Ale or beer became more popular with the masses - it was generally seen as a better choice over the local, untreated, water supply - and it probably lifted spirits for a while. Distilling of alcohol came along some time later, leading to more refined and stronger alcoholic drinks such as brandy and whisky.

In fact the range of alcohol products widened enormously - providing more and more choice to the discerning drinker. As communities grew and governments were elected the most lucrative source of revenue was often provided from taxes placed on alcohol – something that carried on through time, right up to this present day. Many historical wars have been funded on the back of taxes gleaned from alcohol sales in the towns and hamlets across the land.

These days, of course, governments do not depend on alcohol taxes to the same degree but it still accounts for some £10 billion paid each year into the UK Treasury coffers.

It seemed to all concerned, therefore, that alcohol production and consumption was a win, win situation. However, in more recent years, information has become increasingly available that shows another side to alcohol; casting serious doubts over the extensive use, and availability of the product.

The information has been in the public domain for some time and is freely accessible. And yet, despite the evidence, I do not feel that there is any extensive public examination of the facts or public discussions taking place. There certainly is plenty of discussion and anger in the academic world – where researchers, health professionals and emergency services constantly discuss the impact of alcohol on the nation.

But I really wonder how much discussion is taking place amongst the general public.

Does alcohol really merit the position it now holds in a modern society or have the consequences of drinking the product become totally acceptable and are now considered merely as 'collateral damage'?

Virtually everyone I speak to these days tends to agree that if alcohol was an illegal product it would be designated as a 'Class A' drug - on a par with heroin and crack cocaine. Many prominent health and social care specialists agree that if all drugs (legal and illegal) were assessed on the overall danger they present to the general public, alcohol would be seen as the most dangerous by far.

If we measured all drugs in the way they affect human behaviour, health, social harmony and criminality - alcohol would be way out in front of its peers and considered to be the most dangerous of all drugs.

Alcoholic drinks are, of course, totally legal. There are no major sanctions or restrictions about using alcohol on a grand scale. Massive advertising, promotions, sponsorships and endorsements across multiple businesses and retail outlets maintain the dominance of alcohol in our lives. Furthermore, it seems to me that energetic lobbying of government officials by the makers and sellers of alcoholic drinks ensures that any new proposals or legislation developed to 'protect' people from the dangers of alcohol are quickly buried before they see the light of day.

During my lifetime, I have witnessed one government after another fail to tackle the levels of abuse, death and violence caused by alcohol - despite the fact that there are now over 1.5 million dependent drinkers in England alone and more than 8 million people drinking to levels that cause them harm.

What about smoking – surely it is just as dangerous as alcohol?

Good question! The truth, however, is that smoking isn't in the same league as alcohol when it comes to damaging people and the communities they live in.

It's certainly true that tobacco products have been responsible for thousands of premature deaths over the years and smoking, like alcohol, has had a huge impact on NHS resources.

However, tolerance towards smoking and smokers has changed drastically in recent times. The NHS actively campaigns against smoking and provides extensive support to people who wish to stop using tobacco products. Smoking is no longer allowed in public places and smokers are considered to be something of a social nuisance by many people. The sight of banished groups huddled together under nicotine clouds outside of offices, restaurants and public places is testament to how society's view of smoking and smokers has gradually changed.

Smokers are no longer allowed to inflict their drug habit on the rest of the nation.

The use of tobacco products is continuously under scrutiny in order to protect public health and well-being. Most of the larger retail outlets now have to 'hide' tobacco products, keeping them out of the direct view of customers until they are specifically requested.

The general public has become less tolerant of smokers – hence the strong actions to control it.

So why has smoking become less fashionable than drinking alcohol?

21

After all, smokers generally harm themselves - and those who are unfortunate enough to inhale the toxic fog they produce.

Smokers do not usually...

Stretch A&E departments to breaking point at night and on weekends
Create violent scenes in town centres
Attack and Murder people
Abuse their partners and children
Kill or injure people with their cars

...as a result of smoking too much!

Alcohol and tobacco products cost the NHS over £7 billion a year - just to treat the illnesses caused to the people using them. The cost for treating the users of each drug is about the same (£3.5 billion) although treatment costs for alcohol are starting to overtake the cost of smoking. Unlike smoking, the damaging effect of alcohol consumption extends much further than an individual's health. It affects every aspect of our lives and how we live.

I no longer drink alcohol and I have never been a smoker; but if I did smoke I would feel that the strength of public opinion against my habit is disproportionate to the much larger problem caused by alcohol consumption.

Considerable financial investment has been made by various government departments over the years to address illegal drug use, smoking and obesity. But nothing in comparison has been done to combat the dangers of alcohol. In fact when it comes to providing treatment for alcohol dependency the situation is quite alarming.

A recent press release from Alcohol Concern stated;

"For the estimated 1.6 million dependent drinkers in the UK the annual spend on alcohol treatment is £217 million, equating to £136 per dependent drinker. By comparison, for the estimated 332,000 dependent illegal drug users, the annual spend on drug treatment is £436 million, or £1,313 per dependent drug user.

Access to treatment is considerably better for illegal drug misusers (1 in 2) than for alcohol misusers (1 in 18)."

ALCOHOL AND HEALTH

When we start to look at the effect of alcohol on our health it really is a case of 'where do we start'. Despite the huge amount of evidence published over recent years in relation to the health problems caused by alcohol, we continue to ignore it.

Let's look at a few key facts;

Over a million hospital admissions per year are currently caused by excessive drinking and this is likely to rise to 1.5 million by 2015

Alcohol is the second biggest risk factor for cancer after smoking and is the biggest cause of liver disease

One third (35%) of accident and emergency call-outs are 'alcohol-related'.

Between 12 midnight and 5am more than 70% of emergency attendances are alcohol-related

Over 12% of hospital beds on any day of the year are taken up with alcohol- related illnesses

Each GP in the UK can expect to see around 400 patients a year who are drinking excessively. This accounts for something like 20% of the population

More than 20,000 people are dying each year as a result of drinking alcohol. In fact the number of deaths is more than the combined total of deaths for breast cancer and cervical cancer.

Alcohol is now the leading risk factor for premature death in men who are aged between 15 -59

Cirrhosis of the liver has become a major consequence of drinking alcohol. *Deaths from alcohol liver disease have doubled in the UK over the past 10 years.* The age of people who contract the disease is sadly getting lower and more women are being diagnosed than ever before. Recent data, produced by leading UK liver specialists, suggest that the between 160,000 and 250,000 lives will be lost to alcohol-related harm over the next 20 years.

It must be said, however, that cirrhosis and liver failure are just a part of a whole range of alcohol-related illnesses. In fact no part of the human body is actually safe from the effects of alcohol misuse, which can lead to:

Brain damage
Strokes
Cancers
Mental health problems
Ulcers
Pancreatitis
Gastritis
High blood pressure
Heart muscle damage
Diabetes

Alcohol is a depressant and can seriously affect your mental health. Around 65% of all suicides are now linked to alcohol misuse.

Further dangers to people drinking alcohol include falls, drowning, fire injuries, assault, impaired functions…the list is quite long.

During peak times in A&E Departments;

40% of attendees have raised blood alcohol level

14% are intoxicated

43% are problematic drinkers

The NHS has to set aside two million 'bed days' and 40,000 'day cases each year for people with alcohol-related diseases. Some 20-30% of all male medical and surgical patients in urban hospitals have alcohol problems.

The number of young people under the age of 18 admitted to hospital due to drinking alcohol is increasing year on year (up 30% over the past five years). I remember reading a quote made by a leading accident and emergency specialist, who said, 'A&E departments deal with a huge amount of cases resulting from acute intoxication and chronic alcoholism. They would be out of work if it was not for alcohol!'

I often wonder what sort of financial savings and extra capacity would be gained within the NHS and the country as a whole if the alcohol-related illnesses and deaths were not at epidemic levels. I would imagine the savings would be quite considerable.

Looking further afield, I note that global death rates attributed to alcohol have now exceeded three million each year.

ALCOHOL AND CRIME

During my time working in the substance misuse sector I had reason to visit several prisons in the UK. The purpose of the visits was to engage with the 'in-house' services provided to support prisoners in dealing with their drug issues prior to release. Short, structured courses held during the prison sentence allowed the prisoners to address their drug problems and set up a support network for when they were released.

My work involved talking to groups of prisoners who had attended or were attending the courses and to get some feedback regarding the suitability and effectiveness of the support provided. The courses were predominantly focussed on prisoners who had offended due to their drug use - specifically those who had misused illegal drugs such as heroin and crack cocaine etc. I found that there was less formal support for prisoners with alcohol problems, even though many offenders had a history of alcohol misuse.

In fact recent studies have shown that over 60% of men and 40% of women were drinking alcohol at dangerous or hazardous levels before entering custody. Over 35% of prisoners believe that they have an alcohol problem and it has been suggested that there are ten times more hazardous and dependant drinkers in prison than in the general population. I'm glad to say that prisoners with alcohol problems were offered support by the drug treatment teams. Hopefully more funding and direct support will become available for people in prison who have an alcohol dependency – otherwise they are likely to return back into custody soon after release.

In line with the government's Alcohol Strategy (2012); from April 2013 the NHS Commissioning Board is responsible for commissioning health services in prisons. This will, hopefully, include investing in alcohol treatment and rehabilitation on a more realistic scale than has been seen before. Time will tell if this is anywhere near effective.

In a recent 'British Crime Survey' almost half of the victims of assault believed that their attacker was either drunk or under the influence of alcohol at the time of the attack.

The British Medical Association stated some time ago that alcohol is a factor in nearly;

70% of homicides
75% of stabbings
70% of beatings
50% of fights and domestic assaults

I understand that these statistics have not changed much over the years - **in fact around half of all reported crime in the UK is now alcohol-related.**

The so-called, night-time economy' is a also a significant factor in the overall scheme of things – it includes clubs and pubs and various other places where alcohol is sold. The possibility of crime and disorder, with varying levels of violence, tends to increase in proportion to the number of premises selling alcohol. Despite a decline in the amount of alcohol consumed in some licensed premises, such as pubs, there has been a significant growth in purchases of alcohol from supermarkets and discount outlets - impacting on the way people drink before they actually go out to town centre locations.

Pre-loading is the new fashion. People buy cheap alcohol from retail outlets such as supermarkets in order to 'load up' with alcohol at home before going out for the night. The sight of people turning up at a drinking venue already drunk is becoming fairly common. Unfortunately this trend is prevalent in younger people and increasingly popular with younger women. At one time, I recall, 'going out for a drink', was just that – going out and having a few drinks during the course of the night. This does not seem to apply any more for large sections of the drinking community - where the idea is to just get drunk as soon as possible.

Binge Drinking – is a phrase often used to highlight the problem of people drinking too much. Politicians, in particular, seem to like using the term as they see it as a core problem in relation to alcohol misuse. In their eyes if we solve binge drinking we solve the bulk of problems associated with alcohol. I personally do not believe that solving the problem of binge drinking will necessary solve the bigger problem of alcohol misuse. It may work towards it - particularly with regard to night time violence - but there are millions of other people who drink at a steady pace throughout the day, causing just as much trouble for themselves and those around them as binge drinkers.

The last Labour Government set about reforming alcohol licencing hours. The justification for doing this was that the existing closing times of licenced premises encouraged people to consume vast amounts of alcohol prior to the tap being turned off. This apparently produced a 'binge drinking mentality' with concentrated levels of drunkenness on the streets at closing time. So they extended the opening hours of drinking establishments in the belief that this would provide some sort of levelling out period for drinkers.

They argued that with virtually 24 hour drinking people could relax, drink more slowly and this would reduce the impact of drunkenness. Britain, they claimed, would become more of a 'café society'. Unfortunately, the result of the legislative changes was that people just drank more and consumption of alcohol increased.

As one manager of a town centre 'drinking hole' commented at the time – 'people will just drink more and sales will go up. Talk of café societies is rubbish. The drinking trade will just increase sales'.

I don't particularly buy into the idea that binge drinking is a natural consequence of licensing laws and licensing hours. Binge drinking has become fashionable due to the fact that many modern day drinkers prefer to get drunk fast rather than sip their drinks for a few hours.

Heavy drinking in short spells (binge drinking) is a means to an end - and the end is to get drunk.

UK Licensing laws are not generally designed to tackle the real problems of alcohol misuse. Legislation tends to be aimed at pubs and bars - ignoring the biggest area of alcohol sales such as supermarkets. Supermarkets are the largest retail outlet for alcohol sales – but to be honest, alcohol can be bought virtually everywhere these days.

I feel if Licensing Laws were focussed more on health issues all retail outlets would probably be subject to much stronger legislative control.

As things stand, supermarkets are allowed to sell quantities of alcohol at low prices (in some cases below cost) in order to attract more people into their stores. Binge drinking is not confined to licenced premises. Due to the affordability of alcohol from normal retail grocery outlets, people are able to 'binge drink' in their own homes.

We must also remember that the night time economy (omitting restaurants and food outlets for the moment) is not there to administer sensible drinking habits. Perhaps the night time economy would benefit from the introduction of much clearer guidelines and regulation – based on the danger to health and well-being of customers who purchase a known drug on their premises. If we do not address the way alcohol is marketed, promoted and sold we can only expect crime related incidents to escalate even further in the future.

Under the Licencing Act 2003 it is an offence to knowingly serve alcohol to a person who is already drunk or to obtain alcohol for a person who is drunk on licenced premises. Alarmingly – if not surprisingly - this law is treated with some distain in many licenced premises. A recent study by Liverpool John Moores University found that people who were apparently drunk were served alcohol, illegally, in 84% of cases.

Four actors, who were trained to act drunk during the research project, were served more alcohol in the majority of the 73 bars tested in a city in NW England. Furthermore, it seems that bartenders often recognised that they were drunk but still suggested they buy double shots rather than singles in some 18% of cases. Researchers at the University's World Health Collaborating Centre for Violence Prevention said that preventing sales of alcohol to already drunk people would protect long-term health and reduce the strain on the NHS and other public services. The report, which was published in the Journal of Epidemiology and Community Health stated that the law preventing alcohol sales to drunks is routinely being broken in nightlife environments but prosecutions are rare.

When even the most basic laws are being ignored it is little wonder that we are witnessing the current levels of damage caused to people and communities across the land.

Is alcohol-related crime tolerated more than any other forms of crime?

I note that some local police forces have cracked down on the sale of high strength cans of cheap lager and beer in town centre shops and supermarkets. In virtually every case of this happening the crime rate has diminished substantially. It's a start – but it is a significant start in the battle against alcohol-related crime.

I'm sure police officers in general would find more constructive duties to undertake rather than breaking up fights in town centres and picking up badly beaten bodies off pavements. The work of ambulance crew's would be a lot less stressful and more productive if they didn't spend a significant amount of their time dealing with victims of alcohol-related violence. And I'm sure that local authorities would welcome a reprieve from the constant cleaning up of urine, vomit and blood from the streets following the usual night of alcohol consumption.

Of course crimes related to alcohol do not just happen in and around places were alcohol is sold. People who drink alcohol and get behind the wheel of a car have the ability to take the threat of death and injury further afield. Many UK drivers are still reluctant to accept the fact that alcohol impairs the ability to drive a car. It really is madness, but people still take the chance. The result is more deaths and injuries on the roads and families losing someone close to them - just because drivers cannot resist driving after drinking alcohol.

When it comes to influencing crime - alcohol stands tall against any other form of drug in common use today. Police, ambulance services and hospitals are trying to cope with huge financial restraints. Resources on the ground are becoming rarer and front line services are being stretched like never before. And yet we continue to spend billions of pounds propping up the alcohol industry by cleaning up the mess caused by their product.

In fact, in England alone, the cost is now estimated to be £11 billion each year for crime-related problems caused by alcohol consumption.

ALCOHOL AND FAMILIES

When considering the effects of alcohol on the general population, I think the impact that alcohol misuse has on families is one of the biggest areas for concern. It doesn't seem to grab the headlines as much as alcohol-related violence or 'binge-drinking' but it can have a devastating effect on families up and down the country.

During my time working with and talking to people whose alcohol misuse has caused severe problems within the family unit, I witnessed overwhelming regret when people recounted how their own drinking brought their family to collapse.

For someone in the throes of recovery it can be one of the most difficult issues to deal with. The realisation, in the clear light of sobriety, of how their own alcohol misuse has affected each family member is often the hardest thing to come to terms with. People who have experienced family breakdown due to their alcohol problems will face many difficult hurdles and many heartfelt conversations with loved ones if they are ever to put things back in place. Sadly, in so many cases, their families have often moved on, leaving them behind with no chance of reconciliation. Trying to come to terms with a life apart from partners and children can affect recovery and even bring about a further relapse.

I have seen so much damage caused as a result of alcohol addiction but the breakdown and collapse of families is one of the most tragic consequences I have witnessed.

Of course alcohol misuse is not the only reason for a breakdown of family unity. There are many ways in which that can happen. I do believe, however, that alcohol consumption does not help in any situation that is already proving difficult.

It can, and often does, increase the possibility of relationships turning violent and abusive.

Because of loyalties and concerns about maintaining appearances and harmony in the family, a lot of abuse and violence goes unreported. Children in particular may be protective of alcohol-dependant parents. Young children often feel that the tense atmosphere and abuse within the family home is somehow their fault and they will do their level best to put on a brave face when talking to friends, relatives and outsiders. Keeping quiet and not talking about the situation at home is often part of the cover-up.

In 2010 a joint report developed by Alcohol Concern and The Children's Society looked at the impact of parental alcohol misuse on children.

The report pointed out that 2.6 million children in the UK live with a parent whose drinking puts them at risk of neglect. Nearly 750,000 children live with a dependent drinker. This situation has not improved and seems destined to get worse.

The report, 'Sweeping it under the carpet' highlights the plight of millions of children who try desperately to deal with the stigma, secrecy and difficulties of parental alcohol misuse. It really is alarming that a product bought legally in a variety of retail outlets is responsible for so much damage and sadness within families.

If any other food or drink product caused as much unrest, violence and abuse within a family setting it would be banned and the producers of the product would likely face serious criminal charges. But because alcohol is not regulated in the same way as other food and drink products, no action is taken.

We know that most couples will obviously start out on their life together with good intentions and hopes of a bright future for their children. Drinking alcohol may be seen as one of many different leisure and social activities that take up a parent's time. But alcohol is a powerful and addictive drug. It can, and often does take up more and more of a parent's time.

Stressful situations within the family can place a great burden on parents, which in turn puts children at greater risk. Instead of seeking help for mental health issues, such as stress or anxiety, parents will often 'self-medicate' on alcohol. For a brief time in their day the problems fade away as they relax with a drink in their hand. For them the solution to stress and anxiety becomes clear – when stressed, drink alcohol. However, drinking to avoid decisions or to avoid conflict within a family is recipe for disaster. Alcohol should not be used to resolve emotional conflict because the cause of the conflict will still be there when the bottle is empty.

Drinking too much can heighten fears and concerns and may turn a calm situation into a dangerous one. Children, in particular, are painfully exposed to abuse as a result of a parent's drinking.

Sober, non-drinking people can be just as tough on children and their partners within the family group. But we should remember that alcohol is responsible for around half of all the abuse recorded in families. That is a seriously high figure.

When you consider the many different types of situation that could provoke violence or abuse within a family – having some 50% of all cases apportioned to alcohol misuse is astonishing.

Even casual or moderate drinking can cause problems within a family setting. Just one or two drinks can change the mood within a home very quickly - moving a situation from happy smiles and laughter to anger, arguments or neglect. There is no doubt, in my opinion, that alcohol strengthens and aids violent urges in many people and makes it easier for 'would be abusers' to become abusive. In short, it tends to bring out the worse aspect of their nature. Alcohol can have a devastating effect on children before they are even born. If the expectant mother drinks alcohol during pregnancy it can affect a foetus by stunting its growth or weight or by damaging the central nervous system.

On a more individual level, continued heavy drinking can lead to addiction and unless people seek specialist support and treatment they will enter a dangerous and deadly spiral of alcohol dependency. It may sound odd but alcohol really shows its true face when a person enters the dependency stage of the cycle. It finally has you exactly where it wants you to be.

You will not be able to function without alcohol; your first waking thought is about alcohol and the last thing you do before going to sleep at night will be to drink alcohol. You will actually stop enjoying the taste, smell and appearance of alcohol - but your dependency on the drug means that you cannot live without it.

The most basic activities such as getting out of bed, getting dressed and moving around the house will not be attempted unless there is sufficient alcohol in the body. During the day you will only be interested in drinking more alcohol and your only serious thoughts will centre on how you will continue to finance this dreary new lifestyle. Peripheral things like children family, friends and your job (if you still have one) will have become totally irrelevant. If you happen to be a parent your children will be very upset – and you won't even notice.

Alcohol is often used as a crutch to lean on when things go wrong. The scriptwriters of UK 'soaps/dramas', for instance, would be lost without cast members turning to alcohol at the drop of a hat. In fact 'soaps' go a long way to re-assure people that downing several pints of beer or two bottles of wine every night is normal activity. Recent research showed that nearly 40% of soap air time features people drinking alcohol, but the negative consequences of drinking to excess are rarely show.

During the successful campaign to have smoking banned in public places it was noticeable that the 'ban' also extended to TV. Smoking became less of a feature in televised programmes and virtually stopped, except for period dramas or adaptations etc.

It is high time the writers and producers of these programmes started looking at how people really should deal with difficult situations instead of using alcohol as the answer to every problem and every situation under the sun.

With funding almost non-existent for the provision of treatment for alcohol misusers it is little wonder that there is even less money around to support children and families struggling as a result of parental alcohol misuse. Staunch, and brilliant, work is done by several charitable and voluntary sector organisations to help families trapped in a spiral of violence and abuse due to alcohol dependant parents. However, we are merely scratching the surface of the problem and alcohol will continue to be a major concern until governments accept that alcohol abuse is happening on a broad scale within families across the country. We need to address the problem quickly and not hide, like a frightened child, under the table - until the monster goes away.

Older drinkers

A significant problem area, which seems to be gathering pace each year, is the level of drinking in older people. Our population has an increasingly number of people over the age of retirement and many of them have used alcohol regularly during their more active years. Unfortunately as people get older their tolerance to alcohol is lowered – making accidents or falls even more likely. Many older drinkers tend to drink at home and often live alone. This makes monitoring of the situation more difficult, unless family members visit them regularly and take an interest in their overall care and support.

A report produced by Alcohol Research UK in 2011 stated that 20% of men and 10% of women over 65 exceed recommended drinking guidelines and that there has been a steady increase in the amount of alcohol consumed by older groups in recent years. Unfortunately, treatment and support for people in these groups is not clearly defined or accessible.

I remember meeting an elderly woman some years ago. Her husband had died quite suddenly and, in the absence of any immediate family, she felt extremely lonely and isolated. She overcame this loneliness by drinking alcohol. Rarely leaving her home, she ordered groceries and alcoholic drinks from her local convenience store.

The store usually dropped her shopping off during the week as required. She became so dependent on alcohol to get her through the day that her first action each morning was to open a can of very strong lager before she even started to wash and dress. She would then place an open can of strong lager in each room of her house. This would ensure that she had a drink available in any room that she may walk into during the course of the day.

At the end of the day the cans were empty and she collected them from each room, disposing of them in a large black plastic bag. The whole process was repeated the next morning. With something like 7/8 rooms in her house she was drinking around 7/8 cans of strong lager each day – finishing off with various amounts of sherry in the evenings whilst watching TV. The money she had saved over the years was now funding her alcohol dependency. It was not until she was diagnosed with an alcohol-related illness that people started to question her alcohol consumption. The local convenience store was quite happy to deliver large quantities of alcohol to her home and even the local waste disposal collectors didn't blink at the excessive amount of black bags filled with rattling, empty cans. It seems, as a nation, we don't care if it's just alcohol.

People tend to ignore excessive drinking within local communities and are less likely to act in support of someone who is clearly drinking too much. Perhaps it is a sign of a 'less-caring' society. If so, we should look to address the issue as a matter of urgency.

I once spoke to a man who worked in the grocery retail sector and he told me that they would be very worried if someone was buying large quantities of Paracetamol tablets from them - but not alcohol. Both products are extremely dangerous drugs if used incorrectly but they have a totally different public perception regarding the danger each one carries.

They are both deadly if overused.

The problems associated with older people and drinking are increasing year on year and we will, sadly, hear more and more stories of how alcohol consumption is seriously affecting our aging population. It's hardly surprising that there is a growing problem in this area when you consider the nation's approach to alcohol consumption overall.

According to Alcohol Concern the number of older people between the ages of 60 and 74 admitted to hospitals in England with mental health and behavioral disorders associated with alcohol use has risen by over 50% more than in the 15-59 age group over the past 10 years

ALCOHOL AND COMMUNITIES

I don't know about you but I actually like my community and want to keep it safe, clean and healthy. During the course of my life I have worked and lived in a variety of communities – good and bad. Maybe it's a sign of maturing years but I am starting to get less happy with how some people treat their communities. For instance, I never like to see tons of chewing gum squashed solid on pavements (perhaps one day I'll start campaigning about the stuff). But when it comes to alcohol – well, it knocks the old chewing gum into a cocked hat.

I'm not just talking about the usual debris such as cans, bottles and broken glass – thrown enthusiastically on our streets and in our parks and public places. Bad as that is, I find the stomach-churning stench that greets people every morning, particularly in town centres, to be one of the most disgusting legacies of alcohol use. Urine, vomit and other bodily fluids adorn pavements and doorways. On dark winter mornings you need to be careful where you step.

Local Authorities will obviously do their best to clean up the mess and I would trust that the rates levied on the night time economy businesses would cover the costs of the clean- up. But I wonder if it does.

Take a healthy walk in the park and watch drunken people sprawled out on the grass or sitting on park benches drinking from huge plastic bottles containing cheap 'white cider'. Sample some of the 'aggressive begging' that goes on as drinkers search for funds to pay for the next 'fix'.

It's dreary and painful to watch but what is more dreary and painful is that we, as a modern society, seem to accept it as part of everyday life. Why?

Alcohol just seems to show our country, communities and culture in the worse possible light. And once again, we shrug our shoulders as if to say, 'what can we do?' It seems, at times, that drinking alcohol is our main pastime, sport and method of recreation. There are some who would agree with that statement and others – perhaps more inclined to the healthier forms of recreation who would disagree. However, if you were an alien who dropped into one of our local communities for a few days in order to observe human behaviour, you may arrive at the same conclusion about alcohol consumption.

It's not just town centres we need to worry about of course. Have a look around our sprawling suburbs – or the main shopping area of small towns and villages. Look at the local shopping facilities - what will you find? There's bound to be shops such as a fast food outlet, newsagent, hairdresser, betting shop and 'off licence'. If there is no 'off-licence' then look at the nearest 'convenience store' – it will have all the drink you need. Children like to gather around these shops – they can meet up with friends, buy sweets – have fun. They can also ask someone older than themselves to buy some cans of strong lager or cider and then spend a few hours drinking.

Most parents will tell their children to stay away from drugs such as heroin, cocaine and cannabis – sound advice. But many fail to ensure that their kids are safe from the most dangerous drug of all – alcohol. Could it be that parents do not see alcohol as a dangerous drug (especially if they drink regularly themselves) and consider a very mild warning about alcohol to be enough? Alcohol has the advantage over other drugs that are available to children because it is legally and freely available. Children can observe their own parents drinking on a regular basis. They may also see parents acting violently or abusively under the influence of alcohol.

For some reason adults and children do not link the dangers of alcohol with those of illicit drugs. It's worrying and it needs to be addressed because one of the big 'growth' areas for hospital admissions is children under the age of eleven suffering from alcohol-related illnesses. In the end we always seem to go back to the same questions,

Why do we allow alcohol to take such control over our lives?

Why is such an addictive and dangerous drug sold on our high streets in brightly lit shops - next to bars of chocolate and sweets?

Why do we still let the alcohol trade virtually do whatever they like when the tobacco trade is bombarded with regulation?

ALCOHOL AND WORK

Over the years British workers, in general, have developed something of a close affinity with alcohol. I remember, as a young man, I attended an interview for the position of Area Sales Rep in a fairly large company. At the time of the interview I already had some very sound experience of sales and marketing operations. The interview went very well but just at the end of the process one of my interviewers asked me if I was a drinking man. I did drink the odd pint of beer those days and so I said, 'yes, I enjoy a pint now and then'. He beamed back at me, shook my hand and thanked me for attending the interview. Two days later I was offered the job.

When I joined the company about a month later I attended a sales conference with my interviewer (who was now my new boss) and during the day I asked him whether or not being a drinker had any effect on me getting the job. He said that I had actually passed the interview with flying colours but he still needed to know if I liked to have a drink because the job called for a lot of entertaining of prospective customers.

The company felt that anyone who didn't drink would probably shy away from this part of the job or would not be able to meet the expectation of prospective customers. We were continually bidding for large and valuable contracts; customers expected to be wined and dined. Some customers just liked to drink and you would have to 'show willing' and try not to be uncomfortable with the situation.

People who could drink alcohol and close deals at the same time were considered to be very employable.

It was a culture that was not just common to the sales side of the business; drinking was quite prevalent in all areas of work from factory floor to the Board room. Things have gradually changed with more employees now avoiding drink during the working day and many employers developing policies around work and drinking. But workers still drink in the evenings and through the night and this invariably affects productivity during the normal working day. A recent report developed by The Institute of Alcohol Studies showed that around 17 million working days are lost each year because of alcohol-related sickness and the cost to employers of sick days due to drink is estimated at £1.7bn

Drinking alcohol during the working week affects the health of drinkers and their ability to perform well at work. The more you drink the bigger the impact. This obviously has a significant effect on productivity and alcohol-related illness.

A recent study by Norwich Union Healthcare produced the following findings:

Over 30% of all employees admitted to having been to work with a hangover

Another 5% reported having been drunk at work

1 in 10 reported hangovers at work once a month; 1 in 20, once a week

Work problems resulting from hangovers or being drunk at work included difficulty concentrating; reduced productivity; tiredness and mistakes

The majority of employers (77%) interviewed identified alcohol as a major threat to employee wellbeing and a factor encouraging sickness absence

No drinker wishes to jeopardise their own employment or put their family's welfare in danger. Denial is common. Sadly, by denying the fact and maintaining their drinking pattern they are knocking a big nail in their own coffin. Employment, family and everything they once held dear is a whisper away from disintegration. Believe me! There are a million excuses for drinking alcohol – but absolutely no reasons.

There is a culture of 'being able to hold your drink', particularly with men – and a growing number of women. People who are not dependent drinkers find it difficult to understand those who have become addicted to alcohol. I can assure you that the lines between social, heavy and dependent drinking are extremely thin. Stepping over the line is relatively easy - stepping back is not. Those who drink alcohol on a regular basis never consider that their habit will turn into a dependency or addiction. They assume that they will always be in control of the situation.

I've met many illegal drug users who told me the same thing. Whatever the drug of choice, people will tell you they are in control of the situation - until it finally occurs to them that they are not.

Next time you see a dishevelled person sitting on a park bench, clutching a bottle of alcohol, don't assume that they woke up one morning and decided to have a new life being addicted to alcohol.

Far from it! They, like many others, thought they were in control of their drinking and they continued to drink in the knowledge that they could stop whenever they wanted. Eventually the day arrives when they just cannot function without having a drink. They are lost and have no idea how to get back.

The alcohol spiral of addiction and dependency moves fast. Before long they will lose their job, family, home, possessions, health and, possibly, their life.

ALCOHOL AND SUPERMARKETS

"We can now buy cans of strong lager in some supermarkets cheaper than similar size bottles of water" – said Prime Minister, David Cameron, when launching the Governments Alcohol Strategy in 2012.

Are strong alcoholic drinks really cheaper to make and sell than a natural resource, such as water? Of course not! But, thanks to heavy discounting and wider distribution through supermarket chains, alcohol is now more available, less regulated and relatively cheaper than it has ever been. The health and welfare of the public is not, unfortunately, the main driver when trying to improve alcohol sales.

There was a time, of course, when the only place you could buy alcohol was in a pub or the 'off-sales' attached to the pub. Sometime later the familiar 'off-licence' started to appear and now we have chains of them populating high streets all over the land. In more recent times they seem to open on virtually any street where there is row of shops. You can usually find them close to one of the equally blossoming betting shops, which seem to be springing up at an even faster rate. It seems that you don't have to travel far in this country to drink alcohol, smoke cigarettes and gamble your last penny away.

With the rush to flood every available retail spot with places to buy alcohol it wasn't long before supermarkets spotted the profit potential and began their own campaign to dominate the drinks market. They are now the biggest sellers of alcoholic drinks in the country and while supermarkets sales grow, more and more pubs seem to close. Supermarkets no longer just sell food and general groceries. They want to sell everything you could possible want in your life - from babywear to cars and everything in between, not to mention insurance cover for every occasion. They even have their own banks to help you move your hard-earned cash a bit more quickly into their coffers. I expect supermarkets to be conducting marriages, christenings and funerals in local stores before long. They leave nothing out in their quest for dominance. Selling more alcohol than anyone else is part of that dominance.

Just look at the quantity and variety of alcoholic drinks on sale at your own local supermarket. Look at the floor space being taken up by 'wines and spirits' and the compulsory stockpiles of beer and lager. They have manipulated your shopping routine to make sure that you put a couple of bottles of wine or 6 cans of lager into your trolley. Have you noticed that alcoholic drinks are not just in one section anymore? They are dotted about the supermarket, at the end of isles, near the milk and bread and never far from checkouts.

But after all, you deserve a treat – don't you? In 'supermarket land' the treats are bigger and because they are so cheap you can have them every night rather than on weekends. Your health and general welfare are not on the agenda.

Some supermarkets are starting to put polite notices up warning people not to exceed the recommended 'units' of alcohol. I'd be more impressed if they told people that alcohol will seriously damage their health or that drinking too much may even kill them.

Perhaps they could tell people that there is a big danger of drinking too much because alcohol is actually very addictive. Whichever way you look at it we now have a situation were huge quantities of alcohol are sold without any of the regulation or legislation attached to tobacco sales.

Why is it that one legal drug, cigarettes, now has to be hidden away behind roller blinds and only shown to the public on request (good idea if you ask me)? Why is it that the other legal drug, alcohol, can be brazenly displayed anywhere, everywhere and in large quantities and bright packaging. Why is it that no discounting or promotions apply to cigarette sales and yet alcohol has incredible discount offers from 'buy one get one free' to '50% off'?

ALCOHOL STRATEGY

In 2012 the Government published its 'Alcohol Strategy'. Prime Minister, David Cameron, in his introduction said;

'We are going to introduce a new minimum unit price for alcohol. For the first time it will be illegal for shops to sell alcohol for less than this set price per unit. We are consulting on the <u>actual price</u>, but if it is 40p that could mean 50,000 fewer crimes each year and 900 fewer alcohol-related deaths a year by the end of the decade'

The strategy document further informed us that, 'There is strong and consistent evidence that an increase in the price of alcohol reduces the demand for alcohol which in turn can lead to a reduction in harm, including for those who regularly drink heavily and young drinkers. We can no longer afford to ignore this'.

In 2013 the Government published 'Next steps on Delivering the Alcohol Strategy'. Home Secretary, Theresa May, in her introduction said;

"'We have embarked on a careful exercise of consulting with experts from the police, from health organisations, and from the drinks industry, as well with the public, before we made any decision on the precise nature of the policies we would put on the statute book. That consultation has been extremely useful. But it has not provided evidence that conclusively demonstrates that Minimum Unit Pricing (MUP) will actually do what it is meant to: reduce problem drinking without penalising all those who drink responsibly. **In the absence of that empirical evidence, we have decided that it would be a mistake to implement MUP at this stage."**

I emphasise this particular point because it seems to be a very strange 'U turn' from the government. The increase in unit price has been discussed for some time, prior to the strategy being developed, and it was discussed again through a consultation exercise. Most observers felt that the consultation would basically determine what the minimum unit price should be – as stated by the Prime Minister. It was, therefore, astonishing that Theresa May in her follow up to the consultation stated that it would be a mistake to implement MUP at this stage.

In recent years there has been substantial evidence from other countries, notably Canada, showing that increasing MUP significantly reduces crime and the rate of alcohol-related deaths. So why is the Home Secretary saying there is no evidence? Her proclamation shocked health campaigners, researchers and politicians alike. The answer probably lies in the words of one prominent MP who suggested that some 'serious lobbying' had taken place to prevent the increase in MUP happening.

Sadly, the whole mess around MUP did 'much endangered' pubs no favour at all. The unit price on beer served in pubs is already above the proposed new unit cost – so pub business would not be damaged. But pub business could have been boosted if the cheap alcohol sold in supermarkets had been regulated through MUP.

It seems strange, when the population is bemoaning the demise of the traditional pub that politicians miss an opportunity to make pubs more competitive and sustainable. The alcohol trade, including manufacturers and retailers, continually lobby governments against any interference with alcohol sales – citing job losses if the industry is further curtailed or regulated. They never seem to cite the huge job losses that have already occurred as a result of pubs closing all over the place. It seems that double standards are alive and well.

The Scottish Government, by the way, is determined to set the MUP at 50p per unit.

This 'non debate' about MUP is really concerning – particularly when you consider that alcohol is now 45% more affordable than it was in 1980 (Alcohol Concern, Guide to Alcohol 2013).

The 2012 'Alcohol strategy' document also stated that, 'It has become acceptable to use alcohol for stress relief, putting many people at real risk of chronic diseases. Society is paying the costs – alcohol-related harm is now estimated to cost society £21 billion annually'.

There are other sources, such as 'The Alcohol Health Alliance' who state that the personal, social and economic cost of alcohol has been estimated *to be up to £55bn for England and £7.5bn for Scotland.* It is a monumental price to pay for allowing dangerous levels of alcohol consumption. Furthermore, I cannot think of any other food or drink product on sale today that places such a heavy financial burden on the population.

If there was another such product in existence the manufacturers would be asked to cease production or pay for the consequential damage. Not so with alcohol.

The 2012 'Strategy' document also stated, 'We will also consult on a ban on multi-buy promotions in the off-trade (shops) - meaning that multiple bottles or cans could not be sold cheaper than the multiple of one bottle or can. This would put an end to any alcohol promotion or sale that offers customers a discount for buying multiple products in stores and therefore those that encourage and incentivise customers to buy larger quantities than they want'.

In 2013 the 'Next Steps' document said, 'On balance, the Government believes that the evidence for the effectiveness of a ban on multi-buy promotions in the off-trade in reducing hazardous and harmful consumption remains inconclusive, and will not therefore be taking this forward'. Another 'U turn.'

It seems to me that the 'strategy' may flounder before it even starts to have an impact. The key action point around MUP seems to have stalled due to lobbying by the alcohol industry. I am concerned when government 'strategies' become watered down following intervention by those who see the strategy as harmful to their profits.

Surely we can have clear and precise action points with clear and exact implementation dates? If the government is serious about addressing health issues relating to alcohol it should tackle the problem in the same way that smoking was tackled?

If there are issues around crime and disorder they should be tackled in the same way that any other criminal offence is dealt with. Why does any policy development relating to alcohol reform always have to be different than any other? Why do we allow the alcohol industry to influence policy development?

The new strategy and 'next steps' document states that, communities, agencies and businesses are ultimately best placed to identify and deal with alcohol-related problems in their area. Through the introduction of police and crime commissioners there are even greater opportunities for local partnership action to focus on community issues and concerns. Thirty five police and crime commissioners have said that alcohol-related crime is a priority for them. At the same time, new tools designed to focus on alcohol related crime and disorder such as the Late Night Levy and Early Morning Alcohol Restriction Orders (EMROs) are enabling more effective partnership working'.

It will be interesting to see if these 'local' initiatives add up to a change in direction on a national basis. In placing emphasis on local partnerships covering health, crime, social services and licencing regulations the government may see a patchy effect when looking at the country as a whole.

With smoking there was a clear, national, approach to resolving health problems caused by smoking with no room for 'local partnerships' to implement their own priorities or deviate from the national plan. Again, we see the totally different approach when dealing with alcohol problems.

For the record, the other key 'action points' in the new strategy include;

Launch a review of current commitments within the Mandatory Code for Alcohol to ensure they are sufficiently targeting problems such as irresponsible promotions in pubs and clubs

Work with the Portman Group to ensure that where unacceptable marketing does occur, it results in the removal of offending brands from retailers

Work with the ASA and Ofcom to examine ways to ensure that adverts promoting alcohol are not shown during programmes of high appeal to young people

Work with 5 areas to pilot sobriety schemes, removing the right to drink for those who have shown they cannot drink responsibly

Strengthen local powers to control the density of premises licensed to sell alcohol, including a new health-related objective for alcohol licensing for this purpose

Continue work through the Responsibility Deal to support the alcohol industry to market, advertise and sell their products in a responsible way and deliver the core commitment to "foster a culture of responsible drinking, which will help people to drink within guidelines"

Continue work with industry on areas such as calorie labelling, not serving people when drunk

With respect to individuals the government has pledged to;

Invest £448 million to turn around the lives of the 120,000 most troubled families in the country, a significant number of which will have alcohol-related problems

Develop a model pathway to reduce under 18 year olds' alcohol related A&E attendances.

Develop an alcohol interventions pathway and outcome framework in four prisons, to inform the commissioning of a range of effective interventions in all types of prison.

Produce a cost-benefit analysis to make the case for local investment in alcohol interventions and treatment services for offenders

Work with pilot areas to develop approaches to paying for outcomes for recovery from drug or alcohol dependency.

...

The lack of progress on MUP and the strange dismissal of the concept by the government have caused huge repercussions with health experts and alcohol campaigners across the country. Most people involved in the strategy consultation felt that MUP was fairly 'nailed on' for legislation. The decision to step away from 'multi-buy promotions' and 'discounted sales' also sent ripples of disbelief across a sea of concerned onlookers. The government has stepped back from the big decisions and it has to be said that the only reason for this seems to be the 'fear driven' lobbying by those in the alcohol industry.

There are promises in the strategy to look at advertising again, particularly when aimed at young people. There is no doubt that the alcohol industry (like the tobacco companies before them) will try everything within their power to ensure that their products are given maximum coverage in the popular media and through promotions, sponsorship and other events.

There will be renewed pressure on local partnerships to exert their authority when faced with the density of premises licenced to sell alcohol. It would be good to see local health and crime partnerships dealing with this issue quite firmly but in the absence of a dominant national directive – backed up with legislation - I fear the worst. On a more positive note, I am glad to see that there are pilot schemes in progress in a few towns across the country, aimed at reducing crime and alcohol-related harm. It would be hoped that any learning and good practice derived from these initiatives would be taken on board quickly by everyone else.

The proposed development of model pathways to reduce under 18 year olds' alcohol related A&E attendances is also welcome and long overdue – as is the development of an alcohol interventions pathway and outcome framework in four prisons. Hopefully this will be expanded in due course.

Investing more money in supporting the most troubled families is obviously going to help – although I think the amount of money available is insufficient compared to the size of the problem. But it's a start.

There are two groups referred to in the strategy document who are directly connected to the alcohol industry. Details and comments about the work of these groups are as follows:

Portman Group

The Portman Group was established in 1989 by the UK's leading alcohol producers. Its role was to promote responsible drinking; to help prevent alcohol misuse; and to foster a balanced understanding of alcohol-related issues. The name derives from the fact that the early meetings to launch the organisation took place at the Guinness offices in Portman Square, London.

In 2004, the Portman Group established a new website (Drinkaware) which gave comprehensive advice to the public on responsible drinking. Since then, the site has been promoted by the industry on drinks packaging and advertisements. At the end of 2006 the Portman Group transferred its educational funding and resources to a new charity, The Drinkaware Trust, in a new initiative addressing alcohol misuse. The Portman Group was then free to look at the standards practised by the alcohol producers in areas such as labelling, marketing and social responsibility. The Portman Group is funded by nine member companies who represent every sector of drinks production and collectively account for more than half the UK alcohol market. Portman Group members continue to provide significant funding for Drinkaware.

Drinkaware

Drinkaware was established to promote responsible drinking and to help reduce alcohol misuse and minimise alcohol-related harm. An independent, UK-wide charity, they are supported by voluntary donations from across the drinks industry. They provide people with accessible information about alcohol and its effects. They aim to work with the medical community, third sector organisations, government and drinks manufacturers and retailers.

My view on these two organisations:

I'm not sure just how effective the Portman Group and Drinkaware are in relation to reducing the harmful impact of alcohol. The general public will inevitably be wary of any organisation that is set up to provide advice to people on safe alcohol consumption if that organisation is totally funded by the alcohol industry. Of course, the industry has to show an understanding public face in the middle of an alcohol crisis but I am not yet convinced of the impartiality claimed by these two organisations.

Drinkaware has a very extensive website with information relating to safe drinking. It also commissions research into alcohol usage in the UK. They also have useful tables showing calorific content of drinks (which, incidentally should be shown on packaging of all drinks). However, I am unconvinced that they will openly oppose the drinks industry on a major issue of concern. It's a bit like the tobacco industry setting up a website to provide advice to smokers on sensible and safe smoking habits. The tobacco industry has had to accept that they are selling a dangerous, addictive drug, which has been the subject of heavy legislation and regulation by a variety of government agencies.

The alcohol industry obviously fears similar legislation will drastically affect their profits and will try to show a caring attitude to appease opponents (whilst lobbying against any real restrictive practice against alcohol). I never see either of these organisations refer to alcohol as a drug. But then again, that would not fulfil their function.

The Portman Group, under the 'Responsibility Deal' with the government agreed to implement standard labelling of alcoholic drinks by December 2013. However, the warnings I have seen on the early labels are not much of a deterrent and nothing like as hard hitting as they should be. They generally state the basic guidelines regarding recommended daily 'units' to be consumed and some have references to drinking while pregnant.

The proposed labelling, in my opinion, does not go far enough.

There is no specific warning about the addictive nature of alcohol or the serious effects on health and well-being. In fact it is pretty lame stuff and nothing like the graphic language used on cigarette packets. Referring to government guidelines on the safe number of alcohol units is simply ducking out of their responsibility. This makes 'The Responsibility Deal' defunct.

Guidelines for an addictive substance are not really going to do a great deal if you do not highlight the consequences of exceeding the guidelines. I think the Portman Group are providing comfort to the government by saying that they will be a safe and reliable 'watchdog' for the industry. It doesn't really wash!

Such groups should be cleaning their collective act up as a matter of course and not be part of government policy making. Let them show us that they can restructure their own industry first before we start to trust them with public policy around the safety and welfare of the general public.

ALCOHOL TREATMENT

There is vast difference in the funding provided to treat those with an illegal drug dependency and those with a legal drug (alcohol) dependency. This is in spite of the fact that there is something like six times more dependent alcohol users than all of the illegal substances put together. It seems that some people in the funding chain are reluctant to admit that alcohol is actually a drug - and a highly addictive and dangerous one at that. It makes me wonder why the biggest social drug problem we face in our country gets so little financial support to treat those who are dependent on the substance. Is it because alcohol is regarded as the acceptable face of drug use? If that is the situation then we are paying a huge price for the privilege.

Alcohol Concern published a report in recent times that clearly shows the benefits to individuals and to the country as a whole for funding alcohol treatment services. In their report they state that for every £1 invested in specialist alcohol treatment, £5 is saved on health, welfare and crime costs. We currently have a situation where only 6.4% of dependent drinkers' are actually accessing treatment.

Treatment for users of illegal drugs is relatively easier to find. The reason for this is that treatment provision has generally been made available through the criminal justice system (about six times the amount available for alcohol treatment). Alcohol is a legal drug- so it does not attract the same level of funding – even though there are 5/6 times more dependent alcohol drinkers than illegal drug users.

When I was resident in the substance misuse service the topic of accessing service provision often came up during group discussions. People felt that treatment for illegal drug dependency was more guaranteed thanks to the links with crime and the criminal justice agencies.

Funding for alcohol treatment was, and still is, more inconsistent and thin on the ground.

It was often left to local health teams to find enough funding from their budgets to pay for alcohol treatment. There was no clear pot of money available and accessing the right support was something of a lottery. This drove people with an alcohol dependency to despair (and relapse).

As one person, who was alcohol dependent said to me during one of our meetings,

"I would have a better chance of receiving the right treatment and support if I started to use heroin on top of alcohol. Then I could easily access a substance misuse service and have all of my needs catered for."

Not the best solution to accessing treatment for alcohol problems! There are however, some local authorities and health partnerships that actually do put more effort into providing alcohol services. As someone who has been dependent on alcohol and worked within the service sector that provides support for people with alcohol problems, I can't stress enough how important early and sustained treatment is to recovery.

Finding the right treatment at the right time is often difficult. Recovering and sustaining a healthy lifestyle after a period of alcohol dependency is also problematic and not made any easier by society's flippant attitude to alcohol consumption.

I remember sharing a conversation with a young man who was recovering from heroin addiction. He felt that it was much more difficult for people in recovery from alcohol addiction than it was for those who used illegal drugs. He told me,

"If I feel like scoring in the future I need to go out and find a dealer. It's a personal choice for me to make. But for someone who is recovering from an alcohol addiction it's a lot worse. They cannot even go and buy a newspaper without being confronted by shelves of alcohol. I don't have to put up with seeing adverts on TV trying to sell heroin or 'crack' but anyone recovering from alcohol dependency must be driven spare with the availability, publicity and promotion of the stuff."

The alcohol industry has a pretty good deal when it comes to selling a known drug. Restrictions are tokenistic and current legislation barely affects their business. Furthermore, the alcohol industry is not asked to 'directly' contribute to the cost of treating people damaged by their product.

I wonder how many alcohol drinkers are considering litigation against alcohol producers and sellers. Compensation claims for poor health, death or family breakdown could be astronomical. Perhaps that is why the industry is keen to place the blame for addiction and dependence with the consumers of the product – accusing them for using it too much and forgetting that it's actually an addictive and dangerous drug that they are selling.

When it comes to finding sufficient funding to meet the cost of treatment for the huge amount of people with alcohol-related problems, it is worth noting that the alcohol industry spends considerably more on advertising and promotion of alcoholic drinks than the whole nation spends on providing treatment for people whose lives have been shattered or lost from drinking the product.

WHAT NEXT?

I read an interesting report developed recently by The Alcohol Health Alliance UK, who represent all major medical and nursing organisations and is supported by health professionals, treatment services, campaigners, academics and researchers. They feel, quite rightly in my opinion, that public health and community safety should be given priority in all public policy-making about alcohol. They also support the concept that the alcohol industry should contribute to the goal of reducing alcohol-related harm only as producers, distributors and marketers of alcohol and should not be involved in alcohol policy development or health promotion.

Furthermore they say that in premises where alcohol is sold, a soft drink should be available that is cheaper than the cheapest alcoholic drink on sale. I couldn't agree more!

The Alliance has recently produced some key recommendations within their own strategic approach to the UK's alcohol problems. I summarise as follows;

...

A minimum price of at least 50p per unit of alcohol should be introduced for all alcohol sales, together with a mechanism to regularly review and revise this price.

At least one third of every alcohol product label should be given over to an evidence-based health warning specified by an independent regulatory body.

The sale of alcohol in shops should be restricted to specific times of the day and designated areas. No alcohol promotion should occur outside these areas.

The tax on every alcohol product should be proportionate to the volume of alcohol it contains. In order to incentivise the development and sale of lower strength products, the rate of taxation should increase with product strength.

Licensing legislation should be comprehensively reviewed. Licensing authorities must be empowered to tackle alcohol-related harm by controlling the total availability of alcohol in their jurisdiction.

All alcohol advertising and sponsorship should be prohibited. In the short term, alcohol advertising should only be permitted in newspapers and other adult press. Its content should be limited to factual information about brand, provenance and product strength.

An independent body should be established to regulate alcohol promotion, including product and packaging design, in the interests of public health and community safety.

The legal limit for blood alcohol concentration for drivers should be reduced to 50mg/100ml.

All health and social care professionals should be trained to routinely provide early identification and brief alcohol advice to their clients.

People who need support for alcohol problems should be routinely referred to specialist alcohol services for comprehensive assessment and appropriate treatment.

...

I cannot argue with any of the recommendations as they are all relevant to the alcohol issue. I would, however, go even further. For instance;

I would question why alcohol has to be sold in shops, such as newsagents, convenience stores or supermarkets. One of the problems with alcohol consumption in this country is the availability of the product. You can buy it virtually anywhere at any time of the day. One organisation has recently opened up a 24 hour online alcohol delivery service - and more will follow without a doubt. It has never been easier to buy alcohol in this country. Subsequently, I think we should tighten the area around 'point of sale' and channel all alcohol purchases through 'Alcohol Retail Outlets (ARO's), who will, under a new legislative package, need to apply for a special licence to sell alcoholic products. They will not just be another form of 'Off-Licence'. In these new outlets there will be no promotional materials, balloons, sweets, bright packaging etc. Children would be excluded from these premises, unlike current 'Off-Licences' that sell sweets and other goods attractive to young people.

ARO's will just sell alcohol - preferably wrapped in plain packaging. The alcohol industry has spent a fortune developing a glamorous image for alcohol products. It's now time to take the candyfloss away and see the product for what it actually is. We need to deal with alcohol sales in the same way that tobacco products are dealt with.

We must not forget that tobacco products were once marketed in the same, glamorous, way that alcohol products are marketed today. Publicity, sponsorships and mass promotional activities ensured that every adult needed to have a cigarette dangling from their mouth if they were to be considered cool and trendy. When the world realised how much damage the product was doing to people's health there was a gradual (and well overdue) swing away from smoking. Cigarettes are now seen to be a big danger to the public. Supermarkets and other large retail outlets have to hide the product away from public view until a customer asks for it. Incidentally, recently published sales figures on cigars would suggest that they will actually be withdrawn from general sale in the near future.

There are no sales promotions, price reductions or discounts available on tobacco products. Retailers should now demonstrate the same caution to alcohol sales as they do to the selling of tobacco products. It is likely, however, that they will not do this unless forced to do so by similar regulation and legislation.

Alcohol should be sold in ARO's or (at the very least) in restricted areas of supermarkets away from standard groceries and household products. They should not be subject to heavy promotions or discounting events to improve turnover. It is time to see alcohol for the product it is and not treat it in the same way as bread, fruit and vegetables.

I realise that moving alcohol sales into designated ARO's will attract resistance. But to counter that resistance I would ask why we should treat alcohol any different from cigarettes when you consider that alcohol inflicts far more damage on our society than smoking ever did?

I further believe that the legal limit for blood alcohol concentration for drivers should be zero. It's the only way to ensure that drivers are not affected by alcohol and that their judgement is not impaired. If you are driving a vehicle on our roads you should not drink alcohol.

PUBS!

It may be strange but I would like to offer some support for pubs that are well-run and integral to local community life. They are now under the most extreme pressure to survive and countless numbers are closing across the country every year. My problems with alcohol never started with pubs, in fact most of the happier occasions related to alcohol were connected with pub visits. I liked the atmosphere and people I knew at the time never got rolling drunk. We just enjoyed the occasion and arrived home in good shape (unlike the 'get drunk quick' attitude of many today). Supervision was better in pubs and the old style landlords actually cared about their customers – being on first name terms with most of them.

I remember some years ago when I moved my young family into a village location. There was just one pub in the village and it was pretty much the hub of things. The landlord and the regulars were very welcoming and it became a main source of information and advice for me. I met one or two of the old stalwarts, local people whose families had lived in the area for generations. The pub had been there as long as anyone could remember. It was special and I know that there are many more establishments like that across the country.

I never blamed pubs for my own demise as I usually drank moderately whilst in them. I went in pubs more for the banter than the drink to be honest. In fact, when I hit my personal problems and started to use alcohol heavily I tended to stay away from pubs.

It was easier to get the cheaper bottles of booze from cut price supermarkets and local convenience stores. Much of my drinking was done in secret and most people I know who had similar problems were the same. I never related going into a pub with getting drunk. I realise that for many people who drink within safe guidelines that pubs are a great way to meet their friends in a friendly environment. Many people visiting pubs do not drink alcohol at all (soft drink prices are still a problem though!) but still enjoy the food and the ambience.

Unfortunately, greed and a lust for turnover and profit from high volume and cheap alcohol are driving many pubs to extinction.

The manufacturers of alcohol, in a bid to sell more drink, are driving sales through supermarkets – who, in their new role as main provider for everything under the sun, gladly take on the challenge. Supermarkets, of course, have already cleared our high streets of many valuable and unique specialist businesses – which have sadly gone forever. They are now doing the same with pubs. As a non-drinker, I do not need to buy alcohol but I fully understand how important local pubs are in small communities.

Pubs have had to diversify a great deal over the years; building up trade by providing meals and good old fashioned hospitality. In fact some of the best food experiences in the country are being provided by well-run pubs with good management and welcoming staff. I still go to my local pub for a meal and find the service and the food to be excellent. The government has to shoulder some of the blame for the demise of the pub.

Cancelling action on MUP – despite promising to enforce it - has done pubs no favours at all. If selling alcohol is just about moving fast quantities of cans and bottles from supermarket shelves then pubs will have no future. Instead of helping the alcohol industry to destroy our traditional enterprises the government should act to protect the good pubs from the dangers of uncompetitive trading practices.

Most good pubs also look out for those who are perhaps drinking a bit more than they should and will politely refuse to sell alcohol to anyone who is obviously the worse for drink. Nothing like the high octane drinking establishments that force feed vast amounts of alcohol to the drunken masses on a nightly basis.

I would ask the government to act on MUP urgently and provide some form of assistance for pubs before it is too late. Still, if all of the pubs have to close I'm sure the big supermarkets will consider setting up their own 'pub' in store for those who miss the ambiance – that's if you can get your trolley near to the bar!

IN CONCLUSION

There is no doubt that debating alcohol's place in a modern society attracts widespread and diverse opinion. If you see it as a pleasant and relaxing aid to a busy and frantic life you are unlikely to change your opinion overnight. There are, however, deep undercurrents of concern amongst many people who feel that the damage alcohol is inflicting on people's lives across the country is not being addressed or even discussed by the general public.

We seem to put alcohol on such a high pedestal that we are almost frightened to knock it off; perhaps fearing what life will be like once alcohol is not so freely available.

We campaign vigorously against illegal drugs, obesity and support the movement towards smoking bans - but do nothing to stop the deaths, injuries, illness and violence that alcohol brings to our door each and every day.

Is alcohol so embedded in our DNA that we cannot do anything to stop or restrict the damage it causes? I don't think it is! We are vigorously tackling the harm caused from smoking and we can do it with alcohol.

When you consider the facts detailed in the previous pages I think we are paying too high a price for allowing this drug to have the freedom of every town, village and city in the country.

Evidence shows – and keeps on showing - that we are paying an enormous price for the so-called 'enjoyment' of placing alcohol at the centre of society.

We are paying the price for:

Not regulating the sale of alcoholic products through sensible pricing and availability

Allowing the alcohol industry to have far too much influence in how alcohol is packaged, sold and promoted

Allowing the alcohol industry to influence national strategies that deal with the effects and fallout of alcohol consumption

Ignoring the vast amount of evidence that is available about alcohol and the effect it has on life in the UK

Change can be brought about through legislation and regulation but I believe the biggest and most successful way of dealing with this issue will be through a **change in culture**. If people start to see the product for what it really is and not what they perceive it to be then we will have made the first step towards a more healthier, peaceful and less-violent society.

Culture evolves like anything else in life – what seemed like a good idea five hundred years ago may not seem like a good idea now. And yet as a result of highly professional marketing, promotion and sales techniques the alcohol industry has placed its products at the heart of everything we do. As an ex-marketing man I have to admire the professional and successful way they have gone about it. As a recovering dependent drinker of their product I can only feel a deep sense of resentment that they have taken away such a big part of my life and almost destroyed it altogether.

We need impetus and if that is not coming from government then it has to come from the people. The time for endless circular discussions regarding the dangers and damage that alcohol brings to millions of people is over. Let's start to highlight the facts in ways that people understand.

The personal, social and economic cost of alcohol has been estimated to be as high as **£60bn in the UK.**

In a time of desperate world recession and financial turmoil how can we justify this sort of cost to society? We are talking about a figure that is up to £60bn each and every year – at a time when our local communities are facing the biggest austerity cuts in history.

We have to ask;

How many homes, hospitals, schools etc could be built with this money?

How many cuts to vital local authority services could be rescinded?

How much more care and support could we provide to people and communities across the country?

How many new businesses and jobs could be created?

How much impact on the national debt could be made with this sort of cash available each year?

The list of benefits in having such a huge sum available to invest in people and communities is endless. It also beggars belief that we, as a nation, fund this chaos at all when the alcohol industry enjoys huge profits year on year.

As discussed previously, The Portman Group who represent the drinks industry have been asked by the government to come up with appropriate warnings on labelling for alcohol products. Why is the industry that produces the harmful product being allowed to design its own warning labels? The first drafts I have seen of these 'so-called' warnings are fairly tame to say the least. Such leniency was not allowed to the producers of cigarettes where labels clearly state that smoking can kill. Well, guess what? So can alcohol and labelling should reflect that fact too.

I do have a slight ironic sympathy for anyone designing the new 'warning labels' for alcoholic drinks. If you listed the range of illnesses, consequences and dangers of alcohol consumption you would need a label roughly about the size of a standard roll of wallpaper. Perhaps a 20 page brochure supplied with the sale of each alcoholic product may come a bit closer to adequately informing the public.

Accepting the fact that a product 'has always been there' does not mean that we have to accept the way it is sold, marketed and packaged. I think we can reel in the alcohol 'free-for-all' and start to sell the product in safe ways with more information, advice and support regarding the possible dangers to health and welfare.

Specialist retail outlets would be a start - as long as they are strictly licenced, well-regulated and free from the glitzy atmosphere that surrounds most alcohol retail outlets at the moment.

I would welcome a ban on alcohol sales from supermarkets and similar large retail outlets.

Supermarkets have proved over the years that they have no social conscience. There would be nothing to stop supermarket chains from opening up local ARO's but they will have to conform to the regulations as required. I would also suggest that cheap high strength beers and ciders are banned from town centre retail outlets. Many local 'town centre partnerships' have been set up to address this very point and they have the full backing of local retailers. Wherever this has been piloted (according to police evidence) crime has diminished significantly in the locality.

Local Authorities now have considerable powers to prevent further escalation of alcohol-related crime, accidents and violence. In the absence of central government leadership local authorities should make their own areas safe by looking seriously at their own night time economy, incidents of violence and number of retail outlets selling cheap alcohol.

Consideration of the huge impact alcohol has on people's health is now a significant factor when considering the number of licenced premises within a locality. When reviewing applications for new licenced premises there is a tendancy to think more about crime and disorder - forgetting the impact on health and general welfare.

Some of our towns and cities are already addressing this and hopefully we will see a lot more partnership working in this direction. If central government will not act then local authorities up and down the country must take the lead until common sense prevails.

Some of these changes are happening. But they are happening slowly and not through any national directive. Change for the sake of it will never work, unless it is backed up with sound facts, evidence and judgement. There will always be opposition to change and this should be addressed firmly and honestly, in order to avoid a long and uninspiring campaign. We need a commitment from all stakeholders to get this right; otherwise our future generations will never forgive us for failing to implement the vital culture shift that is now required. Alcohol will still have a place in society but it will be a more realistic place and not one that takes centre stage.

Just like the culture shift around smoking, when people have the will and the laws to enforce change they will do it and enjoy the benefits of a safer, healthier and less violent lifestyle.

We need to start the debate.

REFERENCES

Institute of Alcohol Studies Factsheets

Health impacts of alcohol (2013)
Crime and Social Impacts of Alcohol (2013)
Economic impacts of alcohol (2013)
Alcohol in the workplace (2013)
Older people and Alcohol (2013)

Alcohol Concern Publications

Making Alcohol a Health Priority (2011)
'Swept under the Carpet' (2010) in partnership with The
Children's Society
Reducing alcohol harm through the Comprehensive
Spending Review (2006)

Alcohol Concern Website

Statistics on alcohol

The Alcohol Health Alliance UK

Health First (2013)

With thanks to the following organisations

Institute of Alcohol Studies (www.ias.org.uk)
Alcohol Concern (www.alcoholconcern.org.uk)
Centre for Public Health - Liverpool John Moores University
(www.cph.org.uk)
The Alcohol Health Alliance UK

ALCOHOL - HELP AND ADVICE

Your GP or Community Alcohol Team will be able to provide
details of alcohol services in your area. You can also call the
national helpline - Drinkline 0800 917 8282 - for details of
local service provision.

ABOUT THE AUTHOR

John was a design engineer before moving into senior management roles in sales & marketing. Unfortunately, his life took a dramamtic turn following a particularly stressful period. John found that he was drinking more and more alcohol, which put a tremendous strain on his work and more importantly, his life at home. Eventually he had to leave his job in order to address his drinking problem but found that there was little initial support from his local GP. He was assured that his drinking was 'just down to stress' and that once he had time to recuperate he would be back to normal. Not knowing anything, at that time, about the way alcohol can lead to serious dependency and addiction he tried to carry on the best he could. It wasn't that easy and things just got gradually worse; he finally had to accept the fact that he was hopelessly addicted to alcohol and that his life was in tatters.

He suffered for several years before finally securing a place in a 'long-stay' residential rehab service. Following his stint in rehab he worked as a volunteer for the service and then accepted a position as project co-ordinator, later moving into the national quality team. He stayed there for over twelve years. His role involved working directly with people who had multiple and complex needs as a result of their substance misuse, mental health or learning disabilities.

His knowledge of alcohol and how it affects people, families and communities has been developed over many years. Partly from his own experiences but also through sharing the experiences of the thousands of people he has met along the way.

John is now working on his next book, **'A Year in Rehab'** which chronicles his journey from alcohol dependency to recovery. He is married with three children and five grandchildren and lives in North West England.